Equally Strange
Beautifully Different

poems

Gill Sotu

GARDEN OAK PRESS
Rainbow, California

Garden Oak Press
1953 Huffstatler St., Suite A
Rainbow, CA 92028
760 728-2088
gardenoakpress.com
gardenoakpress@gmail.com

© *Gill Sotu   All rights reserved*

No part of this book may be reproduced, stored in a retrieval system or transmitted by any means without the express written consent of the Publisher.

First published by Garden Oak Press on May 15, 2024.

ISBN: 979-8-9879532-1-1

Library of Congress Control Number: 2023938371

Printed in the United States of America

The views expressed in this collection of poems are solely those of the poet and do not necessarily reflect the views of the Publisher, and the Publisher hereby disclaims any responsibility for them.

Dedication

This book is dedicated to the best part of me: my family. To Renee, who has supported my artistic vision from the beginning, to my gremlins Jackson, Gianna, and Lucia who make me laugh every day. My dedicated, God-loving, and supportive parents Dorothy and Cornell, and sister Tessa who, growing up, supplied me with both sugar and spice. I thank God for you all...

This is for the Oxnard, Ventura, L.A., and San Diego poetic/arts communities that raised me, paid me, and most notably, loved on me—1st published solo book ya'll! And because of all of you, there will be more to come!

Finally, this is for anyone picking up this book. Anyone giving it/me a chance. For the almost regular, the normally weird, for the *Equally Strange*, and the *Beautifully Different*.

Contents

Preface	v
This Messed-up and Majestic Machine	3
Prologue	4
One	5
Two	6
Three	7
Epilogue	8
On Being Seen	
...And seeing others	9
Life's Shaking Knee	10
The Burden of Art	11
Generosity	12
A Poem	13
You Stand on Their Shoulders	14
Whatever You Do	15
My Pen Feeds Children	16
Exist	19
Purpose	20
H.I.P. - H.O.P	22
Symbolic Victory	24
New Beginnings	25
On Universal Languages	
On love, music and all the things that connect us	31
The Perfect Outfit	32
Feet on the Ground	33
Around the Way Girls	34
This Love	36
In the Quiet Moments	38
Caught Up—*Part I: Love*	39
Caught Up—*Part II: Music*	40
Peace	41
The Forgiveness Quotient	42
If I Were You	44
The Minority Report	
Ballad of the beautiful and the broken	45
Measure Twice, Love More	46
The Ballad of Oranges	47
On Privilege	48
Black Man on the Moon	49
Balloons	50
Two Sides	51
Best You Can Hope For	52

Chains	53
In LOVE	54
Growing Up Oxnard	58
Da 90s	60
Superman Comes to Oxnard	63
People of Color	66
On Children	
Tiny mirrors everywhere	69
Reflections	70
Black Boy Joy. . .in the Key of Ease	71
Dancing	72
Our Other Parents	73
The Alchemy of a Mother	74
Cartwheels	76
Asking God for a Pepsi	77
We'll Never Have This Again	78
On Technology	
Beep boop beep. . .	81
Statistics Sharpens Statistics	82
Italy	83
In a Minute. . .	85
My Porn Is Not Fancy	86
On People Finding a Way	87
Decency Life-line	88
This Long, Long RACE	89
Songs or Sirens	90
Mountains	91
Writerz Blok	92
Devil's Pie	93
Winks	94
Everything Is a Poem	95
Trouble Man	96
Ordinary Magic	98
Villians	101
Caffine Coalition	103
Joy	105
Skin Deep	108
ACKNOWLEDGMENTS	112
CREDITS	112
ABOUT THE POET	113

Preface

Before we attempt to embark on this adventure, I think it's only right that you know a bit about this vessel & its interim captain. We are embarking on this journey in an attempt to build, to heal, to step off this ship feeling better, more connected than when we've began. Is it okay to admit I'm figuring out these controls, this life, as we go? That we will all learn how this works together?

This book is meant to be read out loud if possible. Give it the energy you need when you read it. This book is meant to inspire questions and my version of some possible actions. These poems are the things I need to hear often and perhaps through this work we will build a bridge between us. Hopefully you will pick up what I am putting down, take it to heart, and pass it around!

Equally strange, beautifully different = Our hearts are not so distant from each other as we think, also, we are nothing alike. And I wouldn't have it any other way.

Your guy,

Gill Sotu

Equally Strange
Beautifully Different

poems

Gill Sotu

This Messed-up and Majestic Machine

This Messed Up and Majestic Machine
Prologue

We all start with such soft hands,
Barely able to grasp . . . anything
I've been obsessed with hands lately
When my daughter puts her tiny brown fingers on my face
No quest or request is insurmountable

As small as they are,
children's hands hold all of their parent's heavy hopes in them.
The strange thing is, the younger the hands,
the more dreams they are asked to carry.
As hands grow, our parent's desires for us
are harder to hold,
become slick with conditional love, slammed doors,
broken childhoods in pieces,
on unforgiving floors.

I kiss my children's fingers often,
even though I know damn well they are all under 6
and I have a good idea of the places those nasty fingers have
    been . . .
I tell them:
I will try not to place anything in their palms
that they are not ready to carry.

I might be lying . . .
either to myself or them.
Deep down, I know it's not up to me.
God whispers to our children's aspirations and abilities
while my wife and I are busy with all the things that busy us.
So, as painful as it might be,
our job as parents
is not to make them simply obey,
but to help them fall in love, with listening. . .

One

I believe we are placed on this planet,
from the struggling student to the cunning CEO
... for maintenance.
Don't matter what your outfit looks like,
you may not be as *pretty*, as you think ...
It all looks like overalls to me,
looks like, hands dirty, knees aching,
taking care of your section,
of this machine ...

So what is your JOB?
Are you a HEART SOFTENER or LAUGH GENERATOR?
Are you a CHILD HERDER or MIND QUIETER?
Are you a FAITH RESTORER, PROFESSIONAL EAR LENDER
or a PEACE OF MIND PRACTITIONER?

The title and amount on your paycheck is irrelevant.
The same goes for what type of toys you have
or social image you project.
If you are not participating in your job ...
if you are not walking the unpaved path of your real mission ...
you are failing us.
You are failing yourself.

What's your version of special?
What is your aversion to the magic inside of you?
In laymen's terms,
why are we making everything so complicated?
There is something you like to do that makes other people
    happy.
There is a way about you that makes someone else's way a bit
    lighter, easier,
Do THAT ...
It may not necessarily be how you primarily procure your
    pesos ...
Even if it's a side passion ... connect with it.

Exact your god-breath into the fog of nothing
and create everything you are supposed to ...
Engage with your unspoken,
until you convince her
to sing...

Two

At this exact moment you are an idea away from a dream.
You are a dream away from a thought.
You are a thought away from a conversation.
You are a conversation away from a vision
and you are a vision away from an act that is going to
    absolutely affect someone's life . . .

But don't get too big headed.
Like I said,
<u>you</u> might not be as <u>pretty</u> as you think.
It all looks like grease-stained overalls to me.
Movie star or manicurist,
the work is still hands dirty, knees aching,
taking care of your people,
your section of this messed-up,
and majestic . . . machine.

Three

Going through a divorce,
was one of the hardest things I've ever had to do.
Would have been easier if she was a banshee,
android-using,
credit-ruining, cat person . . .
but, alas, she likes dogs . . .and iPhones

She is a kind and beautiful and giving person.
But ultimately. . .I knew the person she said she needed,
and the person I knew I was meant to become,
could not exist in the same place at the same time.
One was on this stage,
the other, in the audience with you,
wishing . . .I was on this stage.

I had to do my job,
I am on this mic risking a fall
into the ego-piercing river of judgement
in order to *build bridges* . . .

And to join me on my chasm-finding missions,
I had to find someone who loved me
at the best of my terrible,
unpolished
clumsily leading the charge
tripping over the stones and snares
of my own shortcomings.
I can't tell you how many times
I have failed at simply speaking my truth . . .
but there's no time to dwell on that.
We all have work to do.

This maintenance won't maintain itself.
Transformation is synonymous with actualization:
the peeling of the prettiness of perceived persona
and the emergence of YOU—
raw, hands dirty, knees aching
exhausted, but happy . . . fulfilled,
taking care of your people,
your section . . . of this messed-up,
and majestic . . . machine.

Epilogue

We have no chance of understanding the book of our lives,
if we never pick up the pen.
We become side characters in our own story,
episodes dictated and directed by the actions of everyone who
    thinks they have a leading role in your life.
Hardcover or paperback, thread or glue,
however you are put together,
you must define for yourself
which roles, missions, and relationships bind you . . .
As for me, I will start with my soft hands . . .
as they weather and harden,
I will try my best to hold onto and connect
precious moments and people.
I've discovered, it is my job
to do the hard and often dirty work of *building bridges* . . .
as *PRETTY* as I might be . . .

On Being Seen

...And seeing others

"Dad, I don't like my name, I gave myself a new name..."

"What is it?"

"Hip-Hop Jackson. Why didn't you just give me that name when I was born?"

— Jackson (age 6)

Drive-thru Haiku . . .
(Just a Few Nuggets)

Life's Shaking Knee

Why are you hiding?
What are you so afraid of?
Life . . . won't wait for you . . .

The Burden of Art

The burden of art is that no part of the soul
is immune to a critical arrow.
Each tip of arrowhead,
dipped in self-defeating poison,
 enters the system without prejudice
or sense of jurisdiction.
It wholly attacks any confidence you have attempted to build.

What's worse yet,
is when no one fires at all.
Your attempt at beauty and self-expression is greeted
with aggressive silence —
an audience,
bearing witness to the nakedness of your spirit,
staring . . . unimpressed

The burden of the artist is to forget the EGO —
lose her number,
break any dates you had planned together —
for she will leave you at the altar
the moment you fall most in love with yourself.

Instead, fall in love with your journey as a creator
and break the Ego's heart.
Burn all selfies she sent you.
You'll thank me for it later

Generosity

When holding your life up to its mirror,
is your spirit marked with generosity
or are your heart and pockets still anticipating a return on
your investments?
Birds are not waiting for you to sing back to them.
Trees do not expect their roots to be covered in champagne
in exchange for their oxygen.
God allows us to receive abundantly
so that we may give altruistically.
Ask the birds, confer with the trees . . .
What you may see as sacrifice,
they see as an honor.

A Poem

A good poem feels like it's already been written
Even before I put words on paper
It dances on the dust,
in the air
Undetectable to every known sense
Until you decide you have something worth saying
Until you decide you are someone worth listening to
Then it slowly reveals itself,
like an exotic dancer
Naked and unashamed.

You Stand on Their Shoulders

Raise your glass for the times you have ever felt light
Feather feelings that make you forget how you've come so far
The bodies of our fallen
elevate the ground
Allowing you to see further than you ever could alone
Remember dear ones,
we are standing on shoulders
History has her hands on our back,
Keeping us up,
Propelling us forward
We have inherited strength and wisdom
we do not deserve to have...
Now, call your grandmother back
and tell her you WILL come over to teach her how to email
again

Whatever You Do

...And whatever you do,
Do not forget about the artists...
Plumber artists, teacher artists,
Preacher artists, barista artists,
Mama artists with sandwich making,
rule enforcing,
artist-like hands
Uncle artists
with round bellies and majestic laughs...
Your community is a painting
that is constantly changing

What a misfortune it is,
to be surrounded by art,
but only seeing brick.

My Pen Feeds Children

My pen feeds children
Cute brown babies
Been spilling ink across sliced trees since the '90s
back spinning words like B-boys in the '80s
All that to say, it's been a long time coming
My pen feeds children
Never feeds statistics
Leave it up to them,
I'd be in jail or a casket
handcuffed in plastic, body-cammed and panicked
Instead I use their words to build worlds
Jurassic
metaphor meals out my mind
Magic
Murder any beat that I find
Tragic
Pay bills with story and rhyme
Charismatic
God blesses me overtime
Fantastic. . .

Still, I worry sometimes,
What's the kind of world I want to leave behind,
What's food to a child that can't breathe outside
Is your need bigger than what I can provide?
Some people don't care what you got inside
See your dark skin, but don't recognize shine
You're a star to a world that closes its eyes
You're a star to a world that closes its eyes

[. . .]

Blind leading the greedy
Prayers wrote in graffiti
I'm gonna keep fighting
till the fight don't need me
People dancing in danger
Instagramming to strangers

SEE ME, SEE ME!
You're a beautiful arrangement,
Analog or digital
Your spirit and your physical
You don't need LIKES to prove that you are visible
SEE ME, SEE ME!
You're a beautiful arrangement
Colorful, kind, and highly entertaining
Spirit or the physical
Analog or digital
You don't need LIKES to prove that you are visible...

Indivisible, one nation under a...
SOUL CLAP patty whack
Give a man a break
You say you're under pressure,
But you're the one adding the weight
SOUL CLAP step back
Release the self-hate
Don't it feel good to love yourself that way?
THAT PART
You're not defined by what others have
THAT PART
Just be happy you got a better half
THAT PART
So many things could have stopped you from being born,
You always believed you were a CURSE
When all along, you're a SONG...

In the multiverse of me,
I am a 1940's crooner
Conk, slick back, thick in my hair
Protest hidden in my love ballads
I am a sitcom dad
I am a wounded veteran,

I am an athlete trying to prove something
I am the first black astronaut unremembered,
sipping cognac on a beat-up sofa
listening to Nat King Cole's *Unforgettable*...
What I am trying to say is that every version of me is
    unprogrammable
God gave us free will,
so why in the hell would I allow you to take away mine?
I got CHILDRENS that I need to supply shelter with these
    sentences
Lyrically, literally, and metaphorically
I got 75% of my own dopeness that I haven't even tapped into
    yet
Just wait till I take a machete to these insecurities
Boyyyyy stop playin'!
Now, step away from this morning mirror,
and show the world —
how BRIGHT you are...

Purpose

There's a PURPOSE in your story
There are WINGS,
there are HIDDEN THINGS in your story
There are TRIUMPHS ,
there is FAILURE in your story
Skinned knees and HIDDEN FEES in your story
It COSTS to love...

There's PURPOSE MISSING from your day
Sunrise to sunset we obey
The unluck, the construct...
here's the rub
We are both the master and our own slave...
The CHAINS DISPLAY when we FAIL TO CARE
and SUCCEED TO CRAVE.
PURPOSE is literally the ARTFORM of creatively giving your gifts away
PRAYERS & BLESSSINGS if you do it for free,
Kudos if you get well paid
Still working on that...

Mission is still the same
Freedom through vision
Flight through higher purpose
Strength by pulling people to exalted elevations
Who knew we were that strong?
Living in purpose is like wearing platform shoes when they were still cool.
Higher frequencies
Like dog whistles

Are you hearing love speak?...
Are you hearing love speak?...
Are you hearing the frequency of when love speaks
When your partner gives you ALL their remaining energy
When the only thing they really want to do is shut out the world
and get off their aching feet...
Purpose, is often sacrificing your temporary wants
for your tribe's permanent needs   [. . .]

There's PURPOSE in your search
Joy in pooling all of your experience
And swimming in the choppy waters of good work
It is a clumsily constructed poem
That still needs to be heard.

Your purpose is the moon
Can't see all the angles now
But if you are patient
Stay in the field
And keep your eyes to the soft horizon
Light will shine on its entire surface soon
It is at that exact moment you'll know exactly what to do.

But if you can't wait to get ahead, then look back.
There's purpose in your story
There are WINGS, there are TALENTS, there are HIDDEN THINGS in your story
Share with people the hard work it took to ascend your
    allegory
I'm so so proud of you.
Don't let the rest of this life, this year, this day go by without a little work in something you really believe in.
It's important
It's passion
It's purpose
It's pure
Feels like ego
But they just happen to be wearing the same outfit
Don't worry about it
About other people's uninformed perception of who you are
Understand,
What you are meant to do
Is going to be REALLY BIG to a small number of people
My only question is — what EXACTLY are you waiting for...?

H.I.P. - H.O.P.

(Heartfelt Ideas Powerfully Helping Oppressed People)

Hello happy people it's an
honor to hover in your habitat,
Horrible representations of hip-hop
have handicapped the humble &
hypnotized the little hard-headed homies

It's important to ignite interest
in this movement international.
Imperfect? Yes.
Immature? Nah!
But we are imaginative, immovable and impactful...
Hip-hop is the culture of the
Impoverished doing the impossible.

People turning their painful into poetry.
We power this program with our palms,
lyrical pictures, urban paintings,
and B-boy poses
You may ponder why we strike these profiles like a prolific posse,
Do not be perturbed
We are not out to create juvenile problems,
We are here to mentor young prophets.
See, Hip-hop done properly, promotes PEACE.
.
Dash — done incorrectly, damages what our Hip-hop dynasty had dared to dream,
Dash — It's so dope what these dudes had done on the daily, despite the world detesting them,
Dash — They dared to be <u>Def</u> when the world told them to *stay dark,*
Dash — But dum dums, don't you know you can't keep a determined people down?
We devised which road was less traveled,
and for five decades and counting we DASHED

Hip-hop is a healthy way of helping you harness
the hurt that hinders
and the happy that often hides deep inside
Turns it into something harmonious and beautifully human
There is a home for you here, no matter what your hue
Haggard or handsome, it does not matter,
It's your skills that make you heroic
It's your hunger that makes you historic,
in other words,
to be a member of our culture homeboy & homegirls,
you gotta have <u>HEART</u>

Obviously, I'm opinionated, but stay open-minded
Hip-hop is our oasis.
In this city, our options for survival are not always optimal,
but we stay optimistic
Grafitti writers ornament our walls,
MC's or Orators work hard to create a rap opus to get you open,
Dope DJ's make the crowd go OHHHHH!
on almost any occasion,
breakers, dance to oldies,
their moves are on an Olympic level
while still staying funky like a orangutan on opiates.

Push past the preconceived notion of what this is perceived
    to be
and ponder what it actually is
Make sure that your assessment of who we are
isn't predicated on prejudice.
Yes, our story is one of pushers, pimps, and prostitutes,
but also of preachers, prophets, and then Barack came,
And we finally a president
Our picture should be in every American history book under
the word,   *Pioneers...*
Hip-hop's legacy is both painful and pretty,
but our true power ... will always lie in ... our possibility...

Symbolic Victory

When you,
win an argument
on a subject that doesn't matter to anyone
When you,
quit in the middle of the game
'cause you don't get your call

                       When you,
              refuse to forgive family
         because they shouldn't have said
                what they said
          that made you say what you said
and said parties should have known better. . .

The trophy of your symbolic victory
will be placed on a toilet paper mantel,
BIG, BOLD, and alone
for ALL THE WORLD to not care about.
Congratulations. . .

New Beginnings

Once upon a time,
I planted a tree in a field of new beginnings
Near its roots, baby jasmine and plum roses
The top of the tree split into two massive branches
separated symmetrically to look like a smile
I smile every time I see it
and imagine it's doing the same when it sees me

I tend to kiss the wind in random moments
and in random places
in hopes of finding where God is ticklish
I am blessed for what I have
so I feel I have to somehow give back
Although, I've discovered that depression can often find me,
no matter the environment

In those darker days,
The only thing I can do is lay down
and let the wind and grass remind me that everything moves
and will one day turn into its opposite,
even my despair

As I rest there,
A passing poem I never saw coming stopped,
saw my need for change,
and became inspired
So once upon a time,
a poem wrote me
In it, I was a metaphor for 8am
I was a bowl of cereal in soymilk
to avoid the bubble guts
I was sunlight and a cool breeze
I was tight lyrics over a phat beat
I was no traffic on the way to the last day of a job you couldn't
    stand

[. . .]

My poem described me as a broken watch,
with the word "NOW" inscribed on the back
I nailed the watch to the bark of my tree,
in the center of my field,
and NOW, is the only time I keep

Once upon a time, a poem wrote me
In it, I was written backwards with a left hand using a red pen
Perhaps it was filled with blood
My poem described me as a timeline that drips,
With it, I crossed out a memory of me hurting a woman
who didn't deserve it
I went further back and knocked out that kid in the 6th grade
   that did

I traveled to my 5th birthday,
put quotations around the word "father"
then a "?"
Next, placing three dots at the end of the word
meaning "to be continued"
Finally, reluctantly, ending the sentence with a heart

Once upon a time,
a poem wrote me
In it, I was being created
Soon to be realized in a woman's womb
God held me carefully,
carving inside me, small mistakes,
And slightly larger victories,
He made me look around at all of you
as He sketched out the symbol of infinity
and made it look like my DNA

He then proceeded to tell me a dirty joke,
we laughed about it for 9 months
Got us all together for a first supper on TV trays
as we watched a movie of our lives
with etch-a-sketch endings

Full and happy, I fell asleep
God pushed me headfirst into Feb 25th, 1978 and whispered,
"BEGIN"

When the poem finished writing me,
I thanked it, got up from the grass,
shook off the remaining sorry I was feeling for myself,
and I re-began.

Look Away

Do you hear that?
It's right over there,
I know it's scary, but you got to look
No, not there...there...
You see, right amongst the gleaming twilight
past the amber waves of grain,

         No, you're looking in the wrong place
       You're so silly; you're always looking in the wrong place
         Listen out for the drums, *the drums* tell the story
             Of battle, of peace,
         Of banners of blood spilt upon bloody beliefs

Of pilgrims and promises,
Of God-like *documents* with the ability to determine for decades
the destiny of who will be disadvantaged,
and those who will cradle comfortably in future history's hammock...
I completely agree with you...
I had no idea the right to bear arms included *pens*
That something so seemingly harmless
could bastardize & monetize the hearts of men...

     Listen for the drums, the drums, they tell the story
           Tell me you see that?
     Past that oak tree and all the dark fruit hanging from it,
         Go back a few hundred years past that,
     Do you see where that treaty lay torn on the ground,
           Next to the sleeping buffalo...
      I know; Let's just call them "sleeping" for now.
        Just listen for the drums and the song;
         The songs always tell the story.
           There...Right there.
      That's where they are going to build America...

No, we are not invited...yet.
But we're coming anyway,
We are marching in like a college drumline
Like swans escaping winter into the beating heart of the sunshine,
And this time

We are going to keep watch
This century we will stand sentry
We can't look away
We CAN NOT LOOK AWAY

This, is the most important movie you will ever see
Don't walk out of the theatre after the fancy special effects
Pay attention to the end credits
To who is the director
Who are the producers?
Who was involved in writing the script, and what were their inspirations?
Who has the key grip upon your community?
And who are merely actors playing a role?
Do you know any of this?
Do not look away this time...

        I know the plain text on the screen is boring
            So while you are reading,
          listen to the score in the background,
The soundtrack, The drums, the songs, the voices always tell the story.
    The drums, the songs, the voices ALWAYS tell the story
           They are saying we are HERE...
     This is the spot where the revolutions happen.
  If that word is too buzz for you...call it a "renovation."
  This is the spot where the 2nd great American renovation happens!

It doesn't look like the picture we all envisioned...yet
But this is where the work begins
The drums, the songs, the art,
the voices ALWAYS tell the story
It's time...
Pull out whatever is your God-given instrument
And SING...

On Universal Languages

(While I'm playing action fighting game on PlayStation)

(Urgently) "Why don't they just kiss?! Quick dad, press the LOVE BUTTON!"

—Gianna (Age 5)

Drive-thru Haiku . . .
(Just a Few Nuggets)

In Preparation for the GOOD Fight

Slip on compassion

Wear it over your armor

Smile, palms up . . . Ready

Feet on the Ground

Love has gotten a bad reputation
I blame Nicolas Sparks movies
I blame the thugs at hallmark
"You better buy this love!!"

...Love is getting bullied
And no one wants to do anything about it.
I blame you teenagers
I blame the flower industry,
Which *everyone* knows is really a front for organized crime...

Keep my feet on the ground
Where love is *messy*
And it doesn't think it's more popular than it really is

Keep my feet on the ground
Where you love me
Even after I accidentally erased what you've been saving on the DVR
Where you love me
Even in the moments you can't stand the sight of me

Keep me grounded
Where it is inconvenient
And awkward
Cause imperfection...
Is the most beautiful thing God has ever created

And I want to be in love with you there,
broken,
covered in failure,
but within sight of our dreams

knowing, yes,
we *could* live without each other

But we'd never, ever, want to try...

Around the Way Girls

Where I'm from,
the women were often as
aggressive as the men
Every fraternity needs
their equal and opposite
sorority
And gangs were no
different
Young women, with
makeup so thick it was
tribal
Big hair kept stiff brought
to you by the good folks at
AquaNet
Skinny or fat dookie braids
brought to you by the
good folks at "whatever
hair at the Korean market
you can get"

L.L. called them Around
The Way Girls
I had a thing for Laquita
Jenkins
We never officially dated
but we promised each
other if we didn't find
someone by 30 we'd get
married and move to
Connecticut
Our version of white people
heaven...

Summer vacations we'd
make out while she
popped gum and watched
daytime TV over my eager
shoulders

Sure, it bruised my ego,
but her aloofness made me
try harder
and excited my libido

As I think back at it now,
either I was *terribly terrible*,
or she worked really,
really hard to disconnect
any man
with a feeling of pleasure.
Perhaps because in her
young world,
the two often didn't co-
exist

But I made her laugh, and I
listened,
So I suppose, like a lot of
the around the way girls at
the time,
she was taught to give her
body...
as my present
We never made it to
marriage
I still have never seen the
happy white people of
Connecticut
I became the watcher, the
writer
Last I heard, she is still in
Oxnard, stripping

We both make a living
doing what we practiced
those summers
I, speak about my bruised
ego

She, an expert at men &
disconnection
I miss our talks
And if I'm really honest,
hearing daytime TV
vaguely behind me still
gets me a bit...*excitable*
I've learned from Laquita
that we are not just from
our home cities,
we are from our memories
and the people who have
impressed upon them
We are the time two
independent hands
slightly brushed against
each other
and interlaced...
Connecting, connected
We are the kiss we never
expected to get
We are that look in her
eyes that we will never
forget
And how all those
moments prepared you
for who you are with now
For better or for worse
We all have Laquita...
Someone who made you
feel both important and
insignificant
Who shared the heat of
those young summers,
Around the way.

This Love
(The Marriage Poem)

This love feels like it was made for the movies,
This love...
Started with a quest, a treasure map, and a dating app
This love...
This love is progressive and old school simultaneously,
This love...
It is a algorithm planted in good soil
This love...
This love kindly demands to be swept off its feet,
This love...
So many sparks we often have to take small breaks to assess its danger,
This love...
This love made us work for it...
But man, it was worth it,
This love...

Correction,
This love isn't made for movies,
This love is literature,
Meant to take our time with,
Learn lessons from the hard parts,
Revisit the good ones,
and reread the best chapters to our children.
Embellishing the moments that aren't so appropriate.
Or at least changing them slightly,
so WE look like heroes with this love...

Our love is rare,
Our love...
Our love looks ordinary on the outside,
But is changing us everyday,
Our love...
It is challenging us every day,
Our love
Our love is a Tony Robbins seminar
Exhausting, exciting,
And sometimes, just as expensive,
our love...

We are not perfect;
We will trip on our own good intentions...

But here is what we know...
We will both play our parts
We will both give our all...
We may also slip,
letting pride get a little too much in the way,
realize our mistake,
and have refer back to the
Giving our all part...

Here is what we know...
We will both trust in God over our egos...
We will both trust in God over our egos...
Because nothing this beautiful,
This world,
our friends and family here today,
our love...
Could have happened,
by accident...

In the Quiet Moments

...And in the quiet moments
I see us smiling,
And unafraid
And unassuming
Un-colored by history
Bright in the moment
Right in our movement
When we finally get a chance to breathe...

In those quiet moments,
I can only see it in the quiet moments

Just for a little bit,
if you don't mind...
Can you please hold me
against this warm evening,
...Silently
Not letting our bodies say anything
but...*yes.*

Caught Up
Part I: *Love*

Love catches up to you

like a good burrito gone bad

Enjoy its euphoria while it lasts

After the initial pleasure has been digested

You *will* have work to do.

 I have learned, one cannot live long in Southern California

without having tried a burrito

or falling in love...

The sunset in your eyes

is like melted cheese over slow-cooked carne,

I am,
hungry for you.

Caught Up
Part II: *Music*

When authentic music hits the white blood cells in your body, you are hooked

No cure, pure curiosity

Where's the next fix?

2 ounces of funk

A gram of soul...

A brick of that harmony for taste,

There you go...

Take it easy Youngblood,
don't take it all in at once,

Take your spirit *off shuffle*,

throw on some Al Green,

...and see which cloud you end up on

Peace

I am still waiting for the scientific explanation
on how a leader with no peace inside of himself
is going to bring peace to us?
Why we look to the lives of the powerful for happiness,
When their misery has been widely reported?
Hollywood does not even get the morals to its own stories
We are mistaking the stillness in people,
for weakness...
Misinterpreting quick smiles and soft speak,
for simple minds...
We are, what we worship
In sickness and in health
In scandal and in stardom
Till death does us part
and God, asks for an explanation

The Forgiveness Quotient

If it is agreed that intuition makes its home in your stomach,
And kindness emerges from the center of your chest...

If it is agreed that confidence spans the length of a straightened spine
And fear shows up in the quaking of knees...
Where do we place forgiveness?

Some might say logically, it's the mind.
That's where all the important things lie.
Store it right next to reason,
on top of space,
and in the middle of time.

Others may say it's the eyes...
When forgiveness is reached,
They are the first sign.
The primary indication of achievement
The flood gates open,
and washes away all resentment

How about the toe or fingernails?
I propose they are purely decorative!
What real purpose do they serve?
If they were gone tomorrow, what would we have left?...
Just more skin!
No other section needs a weak protective layer!
Finger and toenails, are narcissist just waiting to be
    attended to.
Colored, glossed, primped, and pampered...
Ready at any moment to dig or dish the dirt.

To make actual, practical use of them, here,
right at the tips of our digits I would store ALL my forgiveness.
in the cuticle,
I'd place my father leaving us for another woman, another family...
I'd place the questions I had for him but was too afraid to ask.
I'd put the time wasted waiting on visits that rarely happened
I'd keep my forgiveness there, until he apologizes

1,2,3,4…at least five times,
unless I use my toes too.
I'd put Maria on the other hand
For the time when I travelled thousands of miles to see her
and she broke up with me on a mountain top,
the scenery was so beautiful
and my heart was so shattered
it was almost as if she planned it,
for sake of balance.

If I'm being honest,
If I strip away all pretense and protest
Forgiveness never needed a space inside me.
We are forgiveness,
until we decided to hold on to the idea,
that we are otherwise
If I truly desire joy,
I must un-cup hands,
Un-squeeze my heart,
Un-trap energy
Un-slave breath,
Forget where I put my indignation,
And let it all go.
Even if <u>you</u> don't deserve it.
Even if you never actually hear, see, or feel it.

We, are forgiveness
However, we are also experts at blanketing our nature
with that which we believe offends us.
Make believe the world is cold long enough
Your default setting will be bitter.

Anger has never protected you
Anger, has never protected you
Anger has never…protected you

If I Were You

We are far too connected to turn back now
Some might say the internet has made us too close
I am merely a social swipe away
from knowing your favorite desert,
your every duck face pose,
political affiliation,
and dog's therapist's birthday
There are no more mysteries to what maddens or motivates us anymore

So if I were you,
I'd love me where I was at
Flawed and all

Love me like we are trying to survive together
Like this world could crumble around us at any moment
so every moment together is monumental
Love me like you believe in my potential,
Like my rookie card will be worth something someday
Like you believe in my someday
'Cause someday,
The lopsidedness of our lives
may need each other's balance
Each others compassion

We are FAR too connected to turn back now,
And if I were you,
if I were you,
I'd come to the realization,
that i love you as well...
Always have
Flawed and all
I love you like before we were born,
our spirits shared the same section of cloud
I love you like you i invented both the burrito and the snooze button...

Compassion, calls on each of us to *emphatically empathize*
To, quantum leap into understanding
Like our kindness,
like our humanity,
like our JOY depended on it

AND IF I WERE YOU...
ah...you know what?
Nevermind, just follow me into this deep DEEP hug
I know, when called upon, your heart will make the right choice.

The Minority Report

Ballad of the beautiful and the broken

"Dad, I'm too big to go outside, I'm gonna crush the earth!"

— Jackson (Age 4)

Drive-thru Haiku . . .
(Just a Few Nuggets)

Measure Twice, Love More

One cannot attempt
To PROVE they're antiracist
So, measure their love.

The Ballad of Oranges

An orange can never be an apple
It often tries to be red and passionate,
But it can never be an apple
It is envious of the bright of an apple's green
How it is loved and cared for by Grannies
How it can be devoured cold or hot
Covered by caramel and nuts
Or baked in a pie
An orange is nothing if not depression disguised by sugary citrus

However, when an orange decides to get free...
The decision starts at its roots
It knows, that it too came from earth,
from wisdom,
from truth.
True, its skin is not as desired as apples
discarded and unappreciated
But I'm telling you,
when an orange decides to get free
It discovers there are seeds of greatness, *inside*
Future trees, *inside*
Revolutionary oranges just waiting to be FRESH

Oooo, I'm telling you,
when these oranges get free,
When they realize they were meant for more than just hanging from trees...
It will be a bright day indeed
This is for all my naranjas chilling on street corners
or in bodegas feeling like they are trapped in a box,
sold on freeway exits like they were worth next to nothing
Homie, do not let them convince you to curse your skin
They may see it as bitter,
but please realize orange skins can make even garbage smell sweeter.
Orange skins are tough because what is inside is <u>so precious</u>
An orange is not an apple,
So do not play by an apple's rules.
Find your own way to be great...
On your own terms...
Get free *my orange,* get free...
You got the juice now.

On Privilege

I've never really been good at good-byes
so I've been holding onto my privilege as long as I can
Sometimes I hide it
Sometimes I forget it is around
like an ugly mole on an awkward spot on your body
But every time you are left exposed
you are reminded of this thing, that is a forever part of you.

I've never really been good at using my privilege to help those
    without it
But you can't remain a rookie forever
Life demands that you play its game
and will methodically give you opportunities to choose a side
to make a difference
to change a life
not complying IS an answer
is a stance
is a position
You are telling the world,
love is not deserved by all
That some people are just born better
Now ask yourself, is this the tattoo you *really* wish to pay for?

Black Man on the Moon

I know there has been black men who have walked on the
    moon
I know it
I just can't think of any of their names
They haven't been on any of my feeds
Not a blip on black twitter
Their names float regal through stars
But no one rocks shirts with their pictures.
No commemorative graffiti on ghetto walls...
I feel lost
I mean, I've seen a brother moonwalk,
but has a negro walked on the moon *at all?* *

* Answer: **Bernard Anthony Harris Jr.**
(No need to Google. You're Welcome)

Balloons

WE AIN'T . . .slaves
WE AIN'T . . .slaves
We are not SLAVES
We are not SLAVES

WE ARE NOT SLAVES.

AT BEST we are. . .rogue balloons
Floating colorful for your entertainment
Ready to be popped when we cease to be entertaining
Just a sad reminder of the party you once had
When your hands tightly manipulated our strings
And determined our altitude.

Two Sides

Somewhere in Iraq
The Muslim version of George Clooney or Mel Gibson is having dirt smeared on their face
They are rehearsing lines and working up tears
It is the big scene
The one where Iraqi freedom fighters give their lives to fight for what they believe in
For their vision of happiness
It's the part where they flashback to their children
And their own childhood
Right before the insurgent Americans do what they are known to do
Somewhere in Iraq
A director yells, "Cut"
And hopes he does the real soldiers proud with his depiction of what happened
The war of men
is a two-sided puzzle
Each side a different picture using the same pieces
Each side beautiful
Each ugly
Each, the absolute *true version*,
Of a made-up story.

Best You Can Hope For

5 to 10
25 to LIFE
This is the best you can hope for

Plea bargain
Betray a friend
Put a target on your family's life
This is the best you can hope for

Trade School
Minimum wage
Dunk this ball
Serve this country
Sell this weight
Walk the long way to school
Or be down with the gang
This is your best hope

Help raise your brothers and sisters
Or finish your school work
HOPE
Keep your head down
And your eyes beyond,
HOPE

KINDNESS DESPITE CHAOS
HOPE

LOVE DESPITE LACK
HOPE
HOpe
hope...

Chains

It is not lost on me,
that the symbol of wealth of a rapper
is a chain...

In LOVE

In LOVE,
I lace my converse, buckle my pants,
don a shirt that allows for mobility,
and give myself one last look in this mirror.
I really need to clean this thing, but right now, that doesn't
    matter.
What I really need is just one final moment to bathe in this
reflection and convince myself I AM what I say I AM.
No excuses, no takebacks or apologies. . .
Say my name

In LOVE. . .
I hop in the car, the whip, the ride, the hooptee, on my bike,
    on the bus;
this is a beautiful day to just walk. . .
And I turn up music that makes me feel powerful, beautiful,
    proud,
intelligent, gangsta, connected, hella black. . .
I'm saying *HELLA BLACK*,
and I LOVE IT.
I require my music louder than you might like cause <u>I need
my head right</u> before I gotta. . .
Clock in, attend this meeting, smile in your condescending
    face, deal with your
Micro-agressions, address this officer, show my ID, show my
receipt, code switch, apply for this loan, apply for this job,
meet your family, and or stop you from touching my hair. . .
Say my name

In LOVE,
I invite you to my family's BBQ; I'll play in your league, make
you feel welcomed in my church, in my restaurant, on my
block, at my spades table, around my children, at my
concerts, *in my damn house*, on my skin, between my lips, and
out my mouth. . .
You lay your pillows upon my hospitality, knowing you have
400 years of conditioning and an entire police force to cover
any nighttime chills you may face. . .
Say my name.

In LOVE,
I can't stand the way you look at me sometimes...
Like you're figuring out where at this hour you are gonna find another hoop for me to jump through. Or entertain you with, or slam a ball through or slap around my wrists...
Like I'm ok for the moment, but I better not dare get any more familiar. Like I, need to stay a sitcom away, a football field away, an NBA court, a concert stage, a car stereo, a manager, publicist, agent, supervisor, and a neighborhood
    away...
Say my name.

I am asking you in love to show me the same respect and consideration that you want me to show you. You act like I don't see the adoration you show your pets. You will kiss them in the mouth but you get uneasy shaking my hand, allowing me in your space if I am not working it,
or even seeing me as worth your time....
I know, I know, It can't be ALL of you...I'm generalizing, DOESN'T...THAT...JUST...SUCK?!

So if you are ready, I think it's time we met...
I mean, I've entertained, loved, served, obeyed, worked for, hired, admired, listened, educated, slaved for, amused, and scared you for so long you'd think we'd know each other a lot
    better.
How about we start with names...
Ah ah ah...me first this time...
My name is Sandra, George, Treyvon, Ahmaud, Sean, Breonna,
    Natasha...
I'll just stop there for a second...
I know that's a mouthful, but didn't I hear you say over and over that you were hungry for justice?...
Good, glad we're in agreement!
Then Say my name...

In LOVE,
I have been in love with my people since Aretha, no, before that, since Nina...Since Fats and Langston...Since Marcus,
    Fredrick, and Madame CJ...
Since my momma taught me that my head should default in the up position, that I AM what I say I AM.
That whips won't stop this love inside of me,   [...]

that shackles won't stop this love inside of me,
that police dogs, nooses, hoods, handcuffs, food deserts, detention centers, defunded schools, community centers or derogatory jokes behind my back won't stop this love inside of me.
You've tried it all,
TRY ME!
I know I am worth every bit the same as you.
MY LIFE MATTERS. SAY IT!

Say it in love,
say it because when we were free, we didn't start our own KKK,
We just wanted our God-given, LEGAL right to sit at the same polished table you ate from,
and we still don't got it!
So you say it.
Say it in love.
Cause if you love your neighbor,
Then you love me.
If you love your teachers, and your doctors, if you love your soldiers, and your emergency workers,
Then you HAVE to love me...
And you want to know something funny?
Despite all that has been done to me for 400 hundred years...
I love you too.

Because you are a human being.
Because your laugh sounds like my grandfathers...
Because you quote Shakespeare almost as good as my uncle.
Because you cried with me when Prince died.
Because...you are holding a sign next to me at this protest.
Because you are holding my hand at church,
Because you made diversity matter to your company.
Because you taught your children our history...
and what do you know,
It ain"t even February!

In LOVE,
I come home at the end of the day.
Knowing now that I might not even be safe there.
I kick off my worn converse, strip the pants and shirt.
Still haven't had time to clean this mirror.

It is exhausting trying to play catch up.
I can think of nothing better to do than to wash off the residue of, well. . .Everything.
But first I need this mirror.
I need to let myself know that I AM what I say I AM.
That I have a name worth saying.
LOVE.

Growing Up Oxnard

When my town grows up,
it hopes to become a city
Homeless folk...check
Crime...check
Middle class pretending to
be rich...check
Poor pretending to be
middle class...check
Starbucks, Target, Subway.
..check, check, and check

When my town gets big, it
wants to become pretty
Littered beach...check
Over-development of
condos...check
Manicured parks...check
Mall...on its way...half a
check
Starbucks, Target, Subway.
..check, check, and check

But drive a few miles
south,
hidden behind my town's
back,
Up its sleeve's,
I see men and women bent
to look like a sea of sevens,
cut in half, picking fruit
and vegetables on our
behalf

They don't look at cars
passing,
they have no place they'd
rather be

Their hands, made to hold
babies and earth
Their hearts, tell them this is
a town,
so a town, we shall forever
be...

When my town grows up, it
wants to be a city
When my town gets older, it
wants to become fancy
When my town takes its first
steps,
it wants to walk towards LA

The cities surrounding stand
white around us
Arms locked, their cultural
secret, their minority
skeleton
We scream in a made-up
dialect at odd hours of the
night
just to fuck with them
We visit their outlet malls
wearing loincloths and
headdress
The white kids who want to
be like us join in to defy
their parents
We give the hippies kids
tamale, adobo, and
watermelon seeds
and tell them to spread it on
their bodies...
It's part of our heritage
ceremonies, we say

They do what they are told
and write off the dry cleaning
as giving back to the community

As we watch the city people dance,
half of us cry, the other laughs...
And as we leave we chant,
Somos un pueblo, Somos un pueblo
"We are a town. We are a town."

Da 90s

Lately, while diligently handling my business on the toilet...
My toddler slowly pushes the door open,
and waddles in.
Gianna and her infamous blue pacifier
make their way across the cold tile.
Without a word, she lays her tiny head against my thigh
She just wants to be near her daddy
Daddy who has to work all the damn time.
Daddy with brief bursts of entertainment
and long periods of absence.
Simultaneously, I have strong feelings
that these joint bathroom sessions really needs to stop,
and I never want these moments to end...

I feel the same way about the 90's...
I first fell in love with her music...
Notorious BIG, Redman, Lauryn Hill, Snoop and Dr. Dre,
Nirvana, Red Hot Chili Peppers, Boyz II Men,
Bel Biv Devoe, and everything Teddy Riley (yep yep)...
you get the gist.

I fell in love with her dances...The Kid N Play, Vogue,
The Running Man, Electric slide, Tootsie Roll,
The Butterfly...
you get the gist

I fell in love with her clothes...
baggy, colorful, sometimes worn backwards,
sometimes with the tag still hanging on,
sometimes airbrushed with your boo,
or the dead,
or your crew...
you get the gist...

We were hip-hop and grunge,
sweaty and loud,
Worse thing we had to worry about from our president
was catching him with his pants down.

Our breakthrough in the 90s was our originality,
the ability to respect someone's abundant differences...
I NEVER wanted these moments to end

But then...

STOP...
1991 The Gulf war begins
STOP...
1991 The poster children for police brutality gets away with beating Rodney King on the freeway.
It's caught on videotape and LA responds in a riot,
showing the city outwardly how much it hurt inside
STOP...
95, OJ and the OKC Bombings are the only thing on people's minds...
but in the meantime...
750 people die in a heatwave in the southside of Chicago.
The block was hot and looked like death.
No one paid attention to the humidity dripping from their breath
Because the majority of the victims were <u>old</u>, <u>black</u>, and <u>broke</u>.

750...
This is more than 3x the deaths of Columbine,
The O.J. Murders,
OKC, and the 93 World Trade Center bombing
combined.
You know, the stuff that actually made the headlines...

No death is worse than another,
But GOD damn,
750 AMERICANS die in the state I was born in,
and I don't hear a whisper.
Doesn't make most 90's US history timelines

OLD, BLACK, AND BROKE...

[...]

Just one of these things will get you ignored in America,
90s or now
Two, and I wouldn't want to be you.
If you are guilty of all 3. . .
well if I'm being honest,
that will someday soon be me.

And my heart breaks,
And my pulse quickens
Because I wasn't able to give them their proper silence
their proper prayer.
Every year it grows hotter in California,
When I am living in the dusk of my life.
When the certain black bleeds into a snowflake grey
When I cannot entertain,
I can no longer work or teach. . .
Will we go back to 90's thinking?
Will my country see my value?
Will I be worth decent AC for a week?
Big question: When I no longer carry monetary value,
who will truly care for me?
I know some of you, black or not,
might be wondering the same thing.

So yes, Gianna, baby girl. . .
come rest your tiny head on my thigh while I'm using the
    restroom.
I will treasure and hold tightly to all of these sweet and stinky
moments that you need me. . .
and I'd appreciate it,
when the reverse is true. . .
That you never, let me go. . .

Superman Comes to Oxnard

If Superman's space pod landed in my city
He'd be found by Mexicans...
Grow up liking black music,
And fall in love with an Asian girl.

If Superman's space pod landed in my city...
Another alien in line for government services...
Another white guy vulturing for culture...
Like most of us, his tattoos would mark his search for identity

Clark Kent would be on anti-depressants,
When complaining to his teenage friends
about how hard it was being so powerful and unable to
    show it,
He would be answered by a resounding "Get over yourself!"
Then brought to the side of the road where a makeshift cross,
flowers, and stuffed animals marked the spot
of another child taken too soon.

He would be tempted daily to misuse his powers
to feed his family,
He'd be stopped on the street with literature...
English on the front, Spanish on the back
Beckoning him to JESUS or Jesús,
depending on what side he read first...
Either way, he would only see another god,
as competition

On hard days,
Superman would eat lunch alone
in the field behind the school,
away from the stain of other kids...
I'd probably find him first,
cause I often did the same.

[. . .]

Under gray skies
he'd spread his bright red cape
upon the green green grass
And we'd sit and discuss hip-hop,
video games,
and the complexities of women.
He'd ask,
"Now that we are friends,
do I have a pass to use the word 'nigga' affectionately
 with you?"
My reply, "*No Superman, you may not!*"

Clark would wince as the bell rung calling us back to class.
Not being able to play sports
and his clothes and shoes being second hand,
He'd often be the target of spitballs and ridicules,
Of course the man of steel is fast enough
to dodge the former,
But *never* the latter. . .

After school, he would fly to the roof of his apartment
and imagine what his life would be like
if he landed somewhere safe like. . .Canada or Kansas.
California, expects its citizens to be a STARS,
or nothing at all. . .

At night, the police sirens in the city are merely ambient noise
He doesn't move a muscle.
Even though the last Kryptonian has survived
hurdling through the dangers of space as a baby,
he's quickly realized he has no power
to fight oppression & gentrification. . .

"It's almost time for dinner Superman.
Make sure your brother's and sister's wash up
We have tamales left over from Christmas.
We are celebrating
Your father finally got his raise
And I can get you the shoes you wanted. . .

No, not the Jordans,
But there are Nike Cortez on sale at the discount outlet.
It's just as good right?
Maybe then you won't get teased so much mijo.
They just don't realize how special,
really special you are. . .
Shhh, keep your chin up,
don't cry Clark, don't cry. . .
It doesn't matter if you save the world.
Right now,
I just need you to be strong enough,
to love yourself. "

People of Color

People of color
People of color are often
put in prison
for not believing in
themselves.
People of color are also
placed in prison
for believing a bit too much
in themselves

Top slot of my bucket list is
to stand in the cramped
confines
of the cells that held those
who believed in US,
Martin Luther, Nelson
Mandela, Caesar Chavez,
Desmond Tutu,
Jesus of Nazareth,
I drop these names cause
they are heavy,
Not for the followers they
gained,
but for the freedom's they
gave up
In what cause do you
believe in so strongly
you would willingly risk jail
and sacrifice your family's
safety?
(Go ahead. . .I'll wait.)

I am a new father I am not
that brave.
Our 1st world struggles to
find zero-calorie peanut
butter,
and their all-world struggle
to save all our people. . .
they are not equated.
So I wish to listen to the
walls and hear the songs
they sang
throughout history while
incarcerated,
vibrating quietly back to
me,
I want to feel the time when
these great leaders
were unsure of the future,
but positive that the stench
surrounding them
would not handcuff their
spirit

People of Color
They sold us a suit called
freedom
but it still does not fit right,
and it is much too loud
We often mask our
insecurities by being much
too loud
They pit us against each
other like the giant hands of
small children manipulating
anthills
We work their dirt but do
not own it

People of Color
Do you know how beautiful
it is when we are caught
laughing together

One of your cousins wearing an outfit they know don't match,
or match too much
Your niece dancing to a song
way too grown for her to be listening to in the first place

People of Color
Do you know how beautiful it is when we are caught listening
When the griots, ghetto philosophers,
the storytellers, spoken word artists
grind the truth into a powder
that gets you high enough to elevate yourself above your current bullshit,

we are so beautiful when we listen...

People of...whips and strength
People of...borders and unbreakable skin
People of dysfunction, distinction, and perseverance,
It doesn't matter how the media perceives our people
All you have to worry about right now
is the story you tell your reflection in the morning
and the pride you feed your children at night
Do not let them go to sleep hungry, angry, confused, wanting...
People of color

People of color, I love you
Our lives matter,
Our dignity matters
Our respect matters....

People of Color, I love you
Our acceptance matters
Our understanding matters
Our empathy matters

But most important,
Our progress matters
Become a better version you
So that future history books will call our people "The Survivors"
We will shock the world...
For when our haters attempt to hold us underwater
They will soon realize...

We *do* know how to swim.

On Children
Tiny mirrors everywhere

"You want me to tell you why I don't like my baby sister? She pulled my hair and didn't say sorry."

"She can't even speak yet, Jackson!"

"Dad, I can speak baby language...She didn't say sorry!"

—Jackson (Age 5)

"Dad—Only cupcakes can scare ghosts away."

— Gianna (Age 4)

Drive-thru Haiku . . .
(Just a Few Nuggets)

Children are a test
You pass by getting things wrong
Can't study, just laugh

Black Boy Joy...in the Key of Ease

We're not all kings
But we are all beautiful
Swagger on 1000
Right down to the cuticle
Forget what you're told
We are not all criminals
cannibals, monsters
Guard your subliminal
Be intentional
Their goal is to limit you
born to shine
They throw shade to prohibit you
So turn your volume way past 10
Make your JOY a revolution
They get so mad when you start to win
Black boy joy done did it again
Turn your volume way past 10
Make your LOVE a revolution
They get so mad when you start to win
Black boy joy done did it again
Black boy joy done did it again
Black boy joy done did it again

Dancing

Black children do not need to be taught to dance
They wear rhythm in their smiles
it is an independence that cannot be stolen,
caged, or handcuffed
they do, however,
need to be taught freedom

To be taught choices
To be taught safety
To be taught safely
To be an individual,
a butterfly in wolf's clothing

My children do not need to be taught how to dance
I will, however,
teach my children that they *should* be dancing,
every chance they get
All other life lessons
will be taught in between the melody...
it is where we hide our most valuable lessons

What you call dancing,
I call studying
When you get a chance,
pay attention to what our music is saying
To the poems our bodies are reciting when we move to it
Who knows,
you might start tapping your toe
And learn yourself something...

Our Other Parents

If I'm not paying much attention,
I often mistake my heartbeat for baselines
so when the music stops,
a piece of me feels weak
Music is God's instant messenger
bypassing the bull and connecting directly to spirit.
Teaching my soul, the only thing that is really important
    in life, is dancing
so I make sure whenever I speak, *my words moonwalk*
when I cook... my hands SALSA
I fall in love in JAZZ
I philosophize in REGGAE
I celebrate in COUNTRY
Every little step I take is with SOUL
and I never, ever, politic without HIP-HOP

Last night it rained and I swear the thunder was angels on the
    beat-box
and I had no choice but to step outside into the wet,
and *dance* like my hips held the fate of the world.
Today, children still sing the songs of their great great great
    grandancestors
Although some parents choose not to stick around,
The lullaby's remain
They will never leave us,
So in that sense, music was, is, and will always be...
Our other parents.
Tucking us in, healing heartache, inciting inspiration, fueling
    a fire
I FEEL LIKE DANCING,
I FEEL LIKE DANCING
Like Michael Jackson's first vision of James Brown
Like a Hendrix guitar string, a Dylan lyric, hell like a Beyoncé
    shimmy,
Music takes everything inside of us,
and turns a plain sky,
Into a sunset...

The Alchemy of a Mother

The alchemy of a mother,
3 parts ocean, 2 parts fire,
All depends on how you stepped to her that morning...
Most parts love,
few parts mistakes,
but we must allow for that,
We HAVE to allow for that.

Creation is clumsy and chaotic at times,
But look at what you have made
World leaders, life changers, spiritual healers, dish washers...
We don't discriminate here.

The alchemy of a mother,
4 parts hustle, 8 parts sacrifice
You can fill an entire Netflix television season
With all that you do that we simply,
miss...
On behalf of all non-mothers
I infinitely apologize for our lack of vision
of the depth of your dimensions.
In the grand and in the details...
The problem with your particular brand of magic
is that if you see it everyday,
it is easy to lose sight of its magnitude

Do not think for a moment that what you are doing
Is anything short of supernatural
It is almost as if...
God had your heart in mind from the, beginning,
There was the word,
Then there was us.
In man, he saw the cities we could build
In you, he understood the tribes, the communities,
and the commonwealth you would create.
We are rich,
because of you...
Holders of memories,
Keepers of communion and civility,

Not that you need any of our permissions,
but I believe you DO deserve your appropriate amount of pointless drama
and soulless reality TV...

The alchemy of a Mama,
10 parts forgiveness, 15 parts
witness, prosecutor, judge, and jury
As a kid, I couldn't get away with nothing...
My mama could psychically sense the trouble I was getting into from the other side of the house,
 or the city

It's silly,
To have only one day of celebration
Do you...know how much,
How absolutely much...we need you?
To put it scientifically,
There is hydrogen, there is oxygen,
and then there are mothers...
Maybe not even in that order...
We, can not do, what you do
Juggling current catastrophes, future possibilities,
your own insecurities, conflicting parental philosophies,
spiritual, emotional, financial, and family responsibilities
Breathe...

Take as many moments as you need to just, breathe...
Thank God for who you are,
Thank God for your service, bravery, and chemistry
The formula for being an amazing mother is complex
but it is not so complicated...
As long as you take the role you have chosen seriously,
No matter what anybody else thinks.
If you love your babies fiercely
And only want the best for them,
you, are doing it,
the right way.
Thank you, mama,
A thousand times,
Thank you.

Cartwheels

Sometimes,
I pretend to be a poet
to get God to pay attention to me.
No matter what your age,
in some shape or form,
we all are doing cartwheels in the living room
for our parent's approval.

Asking God for a Pepsi

When you ask God for a Pepsi
Randomly, someone will offer you a bottle of water
While we concentrate on our thrills

HE concerns himself with our thirst

We'll Never Have This Again

We'll never have this again,
we will *never* have this again
You this small and me this strong
You this impressed at my ability
to simply walk into a room,
to turn my legs into animated trees you can swing from,
To reach things on the top shelf,
To pee standing up,
I build toy kingdoms that you are expert
at Godzilla-ing your way through
I throw you high into the blue of the afternoon
and never miss your descent...
Well, just that once,
but we ain't telling mama about that right?

We'll never have this again...
You believing police helicopters over our house
are the *coolest* thing
Me knowing they are looking for things
I don't want you to ever see
You believing all asphalts and sidewalks
bump, dip, and crack like ours
That houses are supposed to have
bumps, dips, and cracks like ours
Me knowing that five to ten pay grades west
they got streets smoother than a politician's promise

Me promising to get you there someday
Telling you that our rough roads
are simply part of the adventure
You believing me, you always believing me
We will never have...this again

Me putting sugar on truth,
Sugar on truth,
Sugar on your skin
You cinnamon baby girl, pure cinnamon
You caramel little man, daddy's hungry,
give me that baby toe to gobble right up
Where you going?!!
GRRRR!

Fatherhood is a contract...unwritten
With ink that never dries
With language vastly open to interpretation
On paper, still alive...
We are a testament to eternity.
Although I will need multiple mental health breaks
It's gonna take more than that tantrum of yours
to make me want to leave your side
It is my job to make sure you inherit <u>less</u> emotional baggage
than I had to carry.
Or at the very least, better prepare you...

I take this love seriously...
How dangerous this world is, seriously...
How *beautiful* this world could be,
when we have *fun*, taking it, *seriously*
And we only have these brief moments to get ALL this done.
So on the days I squeeze you longer and tighter than your
boundless energy will entertain
Just allow me this quiet vulnerability for a moment.
We'll never have this exact US, again...

Let's go to the place where you don't hurt,
and I don't work
The place in the picture we love,
that freezes the sunlight on our faces
and the youth in our bodies
Pause that part of the video
In the middle of your dance
mid-thrust, mid-air, off-beat,
the indivisible, undeniable
You and me
And I know we can't stay here forever little one
Even in this digital age,
we get lost in the hard drives of our need for individual
ambitions...
But for this moment little one,
I'm pretending time passed us by
like the turtle shaped clouds you like to point out...
And now...
I'm about to gobble all them little toes right up...Grrrr

[...]

How long will you <u>long</u> for me to be your monster?
How long will it take you to find the sword of puberty
and you consider me. . .a monster?
How many mistakes do I get in raising you?
In disappointing your mother?

What if I just say NO?
you are not allowed to leave this moment
To grow into another body
To get too heavy to lift you over the crowd,
so that you can see what is coming,
so that the *only* thing you have to deal with is your imagination,
and that's still filled with furry neon,
and sweet things that make your mouth and hands sticky
and I got backpacks and several diaper bags full of sugar. . .
Not that sweet and low stuff either,
I'm talking *pure cane sugar. . .*

Sugar on truth,
sugar on your skin,
you cinnamon baby girl,
pure sweet, *spicy* cinnamon
I want you *yell that* to any insecurity that questions you. . .
You caramel little man,
daddy's hungry,
Give me that disillusionment to gobble right up. . .
Kids, we don't have to leave this castle
until we want to. . .Okay?
Let's just sit here, and pretend time,
forgot us. . .

On Technology
Beep boop beep...

(*After giving me an unsolicited and sincere hug.*)

"Daddy, thank you for letting me watch *Ninja Turtles*, It helps me learn how to beat you."
—Jackson (Age 6)

[* *author's note: I believe he was dead serious.*]

Drive-thru Haiku . . .
(Just a Few Nuggets)

Statistics Sharpen Statistics

You got statistics

I got counter statistics

Who wins, if love fails?

Italy

Sitting in the middle of history
Archaic buildings that have withstood
all that time has had time to throw at it
I'm capturing moments with technology
This iPhone will have to be replaced in about a year
100 lunar cycles later,
these monuments and statues *will still be here*
So it begs the question,
APPLE or MICHAELANGELO
Which thinking is truly more advanced?

Being Social—Anti or Otherwise

Feel it
Compose it
Post-it
Regret it

Edit it
Repost it
Defend it
Forget it

While working very hard,
To remind the world that you exist
Do not ignore the evidence
That *the world*
. . .is in you.

In a Minute. . .

Browsing social media
is like flipping through a large coloring book
of all the adventures you are NOT having in your life

The most you can do
is comment on the caption in crayon
Tell the characters how wonderful it is
that they are so wonderful
Congratulate the princess for being a princess
High five the knight for slaying his dragon

And while the *real world* waits patiently
for you to get to know her
You hold up a finger to her while scrolling,
"In a minute," you say,
"Just one more minute. . ."

My Porn Is Not Fancy

My porn is not fancy
Hold on...Siri just wrote down "porn" instead of "poem"...
Allow me to start again

My POEM is not fancy
It will not make you jump out your seat
and breakdance down the aisle

My poem loves you...
but has a hard time expressing itself
My poem is not "Dope" or "Sick"
Does not go viral or contain a virus
It is hot tea and reflection on the afternoon of Dec 25th,
after the presents have been opened and you realize
people don't know you at all...

My poem is an unexpected call from an unexpected person
My poem is like a murder...
Wait a second...damn autocorrect wrote down "Murder"
instead of "Moment" and I memorized it that way

Let me start again
My poem is a moment
My poem is a mistake and living with it
My poem is an apology to better poems
My poem keeps all the bad and squishy stuff in, like spandex
My poem is a superhero with bad weekend box office grosses
Saving one spirit at time,
for as long as it can...

On People Finding a Way

"Dad, what's the point of a bath? You get wet, then you get dry again...I'm already dry!!"

—Jackson (Age 4)

"Dad, can I have some candy? Mom said no..."

—Gianna (Age 4)

Drive-thru Haiku . . .
(Just a Few Nuggets)

Decency life-line

Decency survives
Less in keyboards, more in eyes
There's no app for that.

This Long, Long RACE

When you set out to make a difference
You are bound by red tape
And asked to awkwardly run a race
where it feels like cheering only happens
when you appear to be failing

When you set out to make a difference
The announcer mispronounces your name
He speaks as if you have already lost

But each lap you complete,
Someone smiles in recognition
Another begins running clumsily behind you
Even more are being infused with inspiration
without them even realizing it

You are making a difference
Even if each step you attempt does not *feel* different
Even if they inspect and respect your degrees
before they do your heart,
what you are trying to do for them,
Or the path you are trying to clear
Do not mistake a *hard road* for one void of value
You are making a difference
You are becoming, the difference

How wonderful is it to know,
That at the end of this race
The trail of light you leave behind
Will illuminate a path for those coming after you
That is how decency works
That is how the sun works
That is how love works

Songs or Sirens

As the newscaster spins her description of the crime
the cameraman begins to lose focus
He just found out he is to be a father
In between segments, the reporter asks about the condition of her hair
Cameraman is thinking of names,
ones that will match his wife's eyes
They are like pools, he;
will teach his new son or daughter to swim
In his earpiece he hears the next segment will be about a fatal accident
But he daydreams about how simultaneously happy and gross it will be
seeing his wife give birth
Today, nothing can keep his feet on the ground, not even life

It is possible outside of the Matrix to control your reality
Ask any celebrity; perception is everything,
Happiness belongs to the dreamers
Those who see a broom handle but imagines a microphone
Those who can see a blank screen and fill it with a literary kingdom
Those who can turn their arms into wings,
What is happiness if not flight, real or imagined
If the earth is really suspended in space right now
are we walking, or are we flying?
A song, is nothing but vibrations with good intentions
It does not die when the iPod is turned off
Neither does the newscasters voice when describing the crime
Which do you choose to hold on to. . .
The songs in your life, or the police sirens
To what do you wish to spend the currency of your time?
Buying into bitterness is like pre-ordering death and disappointment on Amazon. . .
A happy fool is invited to the party
The realist stays at home and calls the cops,
when the laughter becomes unbearable.

Mountains

And at the heart of the matter
    No matter what direction we face
    The mountain still stands, cold, looming
Let's walk to the river, you say
    Things sparkle in the river,
    Life is softer at the river

No amount of negotiating or avoidance
    will turn the mountain into a speed bump,
Your fears into fairytales
    Or your pain into peace
    We must stand in front of that which blocks our view of
        the sun,
and climb until our legs are weak,
but our heart is strong
    Until we can tower on top of that obstacle,
exhausted, sweating,
knowing. . .
It will never, ever, overcome us, again

Writerz Blok

We paint, with blue struggle and orange triumph
We tag, our brown essence into white histories
We mural, neon hip-hop into gray cultures
We graph, red love on these ash streets
We teach, green youth to see themselves… as gold
Our mission, is to illuminate pathways with bright colors
To empower though artwork,
so our young
become works of art

Devil's Pie

I am a dark coyote in a bright city
Just looking for something soft. . .
Lived in the desert,
but I am attracted to neon lights and hip-hop beats
Alcohol washes my sins and cleans my fur
Both the city and the desert is hard
And I'm just looking for something soft. . .

This bright city is full of dark kittens
wanting something wild
They are poets,
purring for a high
Don't have the heart or the conscious to explain the theory of gravity
That anything that is not made for the sky
starts to get heavy
Fuck it, what do I care anyway, I'm a coyote
Looking for something soft

When I'm not hunting, I'm watching TV
I skip the shows and just commercial surf
I'm in love with beautiful liars
and sexy words
that blanket ugly intentions
So me and commercials get along just fine

Near my bed there are bibles,
I let kittens guess at my motivations
They believe a book says something about me
But books don't talk honey
Only teeth and tongues
And this mouth. . .is just looking for something soft

I love young men with full eyes and empty stomachs
I show them pictures of smiling people holding shiny things
and they begin to moan. . .
I show them fast things
and hear their stomachs rumble
Keep them so hot and hungry they become coyotes too
I need friends;
everyone, needs friends.

Winks

When a homeless man winks at you,
You instantly feel as though you have been left out of a huge secret
Your mind races to all the classes you fell asleep in
All the parental advice you have actively ignored

As discreet as possible,
you check the homeless man for wings
Maybe this is a test?
Perhaps this is a warning?
Seriously homeboy...what's up with the WINK?!!
To be quite honest,
a homeless wink kinda fucks you up...

Everything Is a Poem

Everything is a poem,
If you want it to be
Including, but not limited to:
Rain on a picnic
A scar that won't heal
Losing someone,
just when they have found their way into your heart

Everybody is a poem,
If you seek the beauty in them
Including but not limited to:
Big-boned people who think they are skinny
Skinny people who think they are fat
Medium-sized people who are never satisfied with their reflection

Everyone is a poem,
If they decide to become one
A woman, deciding that she was not an actress
and that this was the last time she would play the role
of someone's punching bag
A young boy, challenging Webster's dictionary's definition of the adjective "BLACK"
and manipulating it in his spirit to mean "BEAUTIFUL" and "FULL OF DEPTH"

Or you...on that day you decided you had more to offer the world
and took one more timid step
towards the person you were supposed to be.
You remember that day right?
Let me tell you,
you were absolutely *beautiful* in that moment.
Poetic...

I had no choice in becoming a poet,
because I saw poems everywhere.
And I must admit, as a man, I'm ok,
...But as a poem, I'm damn dope!!!

Trouble Man

In my neighborhood, we had a supervillain...
Smarter than Lex Luthor
More sadistic than the Joker
Older than Magneto
He is the many-faced god,
With more kung fu skills than the Shedder
I call him TROUBLE-MAN

Trouble-man would terrorize my neighborhood by raising
    rents,
Gossiping,
Getting good folks laid off
and hooked on chemical escape

As well as keeping my father away for months at a time

Trouble-man is a lie...
Trouble-man, he stay busy...
They say Trouble-man was a slave turned <u>slaver</u>
Trouble-man so bad had white men tell <u>him</u> "Yes Sir"

But no one ever see trouble-man
Trouble-man's never a shout
Trouble-man's a whisper
In fact, he whisper so good,
he make you want to shout

"Ha!" James Brown knew him
"Hee-he" Michael Jackson knew him
For some reason he's always trying
to get Black men to perm their hair...
But he don't care about your skin,
He just like the taste of your soul,

He even got to Martin...Luther...King...
When times were hard...
And Coretta was far...
And you could taste the lust and the heat in the air in
Mississippi,
Memphis, Birmingham...

That's where Trouble-man stay,
In any country, ghetto, or barrio, USA
He likes to live in the heat...
And the lust...
And he whisper...
Rubbing your back softly,
he whispers...
About to do everything you ain't supposed to be doing,
he whispers...
Two words most dangerous in the English language...
Smiling,
With our ears hungry,
And his words, sweet...
He whispers,
"FUCK IT..."

Ordinary Magic
(short version)

It must be magic,
cause no one can tell me how love really works
How it is able to die daily online and reincarnate in the belly
of a laugh
An unexpected embrace
An anticipated 1st kiss
Tell me, there isn't *magic* in this. . .

It must be magic because my parents met when they were 11
divorced when I was 11
And remarried when I was 34.
I am now 11 anew
. . .still wearing transformers t-shirts
Excited again to see my parents hold hands, once more

Speaking of children and magic
magic and children
My first child Jackson, he is less than a year old
Wears Batman and swells his chest
Protects his mother
As his father did at his age
I too was the Dark Knight
Who didn't require the night to be dark
Codename: Chocolate Avenger!!

My father took it one step further,
squeezed into his sister's ballerina tights
and also played the role of the caped crusader
Three generations of superheroes
Pretending to be the good guy
We all now use language to fight injustice
My father, a high school councilor
I, a socially conscience playwright & poet
My son, shrieks when he laughs
And when he does, depression suddenly dematerializes from
    our home
I imagine a big cartoon PLOW! or BAM! above his head when
    this happens. . .
Tell me there isn't *magic* in this

Why is this important
Because Ordinary Magic is being forgotten at an alarming rate

I know there are proud nerds listening
who do not care much for poetry
So here is a John Hopkins statistic,
Lisa Yanek M.P.H. has found that positive people
are 13% less likely than their negative counterparts
to have a heart attack or other coronary event.

Dr. Peterson at the University of Michigan has found,
that people whose explanatory style is pessimistic
exercise less and smoke and drink more than do optimists.

Edward E. Jones, a psychologist at Princeton University says,
"Our expectancies not only affect how we see reality
but also affect the reality itself,"

. . .and *Maxim* magazine claims if you are positive,
you'll just have more sex

So there you have it
Ordinary magic
I see it everywhere
Hiding in plain sight
Loving for no good reason
A black man with no fancy education speaking to you good people here at a TEDx
Armed only with a disturbingly handsome face
And a pocket full of passion
Ten years ago, I could barely afford Ramen
Now for a living I write pretty words and married an even prettier frugal woman
And people no longer laugh at my credit score. . .

We must change the definition of what is miraculous
Disney will have you believe it happens instantaneous,
And in a way it does,
But, it is doesn't just happen with the snap of the fingers or by evoking incantations. . .

[. . .]

This type of wizardry happens in the heart of a realization
True sorcery begins the MOMENT you recognize
that sometime in your life you have gone through a version of absolute hell, and somehow...survived
And if need be, you can do it again
Now tell me
there isn't magic in that?

Villians

The mind is a funny thing...
Not funny "HA HA" but funny "God damn."
The mind will forget names, faces...
I haven't memorized a phone number besides mine since
    1996.
It is also rather easy to forget times when you are happy.
That you should be happy now
That compared to most in this world,
you have the MOST in this world
I am excellent at forgetting that.
I'm an Olympic athlete at forgetting I should be happy,
grateful...

I don't forget shame though
I can't forget high school
And the classroom
That it was sunny
And I was competing to outshine the sky
to hide some of my dark
So I chose a female who was darker,
Hair more nappy, stomach more extended
I whispered about her so my friends would chuckle
I chuckled so that my friends would laugh out loud
I laughed so my friends would attack
And safe from my perch I watched,
wishing I remembered the command to make them stop
Wishing I remembered how to summon the same courage it
took to start the bullying and use it to end it.

But the mind is a funny thing
Not funny "HA HA" but funny, "I'm sorry."
And that was all I could say, "I'm sorry."
Ironically placing my arm around the girl I helped hurt

The world's greatest villains do not start out as villains.
They are not the bully's of the world
They are the ones crying outside of classrooms,
In corners where you can scarcely see them
They are the ones you do not notice until it is too late
While you are trying hard to outshine the sun,
                                                      [...]

they grow dark in your shadow
There is someone, in every room you enter,
For fear of too much light,
that will not speak to anyone entering,
and will not speak upon exiting...
When you find them,
Ask them what they do or what do they dream,
they will do the same for you
There may be an Alexander Luther
that is on the verge of becoming Lex.
A Wilson Fisk, one poisonous interaction away
from becoming a Kingpin.

I'm telling you the mind is a funny thing,
Not funny "HA HA" but funny,
"Why is it so damn hard, for us to be decent to one another?"

Caffine Coalition

We all, want this to work...
This, experiment of United, States...
A coalition of colors, cultures, convictions,
and low key addiction to caffeine.

I wrote this poem in a Starbucks
I wrote this poem overhearing conversations,
soft rock, remote work, and folks concentrating on their
    dreams.
I wrote this sitting between a homeless man
hoping not to get kicked out,
And a woman on a $2000 MacBook Pro
I wrote this poem in the middle of suburbia
with images beckoning us back to nature on the wall behind
    us.
We are walking, texting, scrolling, posting contradictions...
But we ALL need this, to work...

What is our together?
What's the thing that's going to unite us besides another
    9/11?
What is our communal cause when our ideologies can be so
    radically different?
I contend that kindness is not controversial
Respect has no political affiliation until you give her one.
I know it all sounds corny,
but how we show up in a space matters
The genesis of equity is conversation
Deep, meaningful, progressive, *anti-pointless* conversations are
deathly allergic to self-righteousness, anger,
or the idea that *your* point of view is our *only* path

The pop sorcerer Michael Jackson once evoked,
"mama se mama sa mama coo sa" which translates roughly into.

Listen more than you think, think more than you speak and when all
else fails...you better dance! (Don't fact check me on that
    though.)

[...]

It is really hard to listen without having your rebuttal locked
    and loaded.
It's a radical act to fundamentally disagree
and still treat said person with common decency.

The big question is,
are you currently, internally, actively
trying NOT to be divided?...
Or is your blanket, your comfort,
to "other" us back into segregation?

We ALL want this to work...
For this harvest of humans to yield sustenance
and equality of opportunity.
A field of dreamers
A sky of souls,
Beautiful in our vast complexity,
The interconnectedness of bio-luminary diversity
I see you shining
I see you being a light
I see you starting the conversation
I see you giving people voice
I see you caring about the answers
I see you caring about the answers
I see you caring about the answers
I see you loving despite differences
Harnessing humanity instead of hurling hate

That is the beginning of our together
The untangling of the thread to start to see what actually
connects us
Crazy in our belief that WE can make this work
A coalition of colors, cultures and convictions
A common unity
With a low key, barely noticeable,
we can quit anytime, addiction to caffeine...
But that's ok...
Because we *HAVE* to be the energy,
this movement needs

Joy

I believe in joy
I believe in joy like my mother believes
that prayer is the strongest armor a person can put on
Like my son believes
I am literally the strongest person in the world
Like my wife strongly believes
that there are always chores that can be done...
Even on Sunday

I believe joy is inherent,
but very easy to unlearn
I believe joy is inherent,
but unrecognizable in an Instagram lineup
I believe joy is inherently a part of us,
But is diluted when the choices we make
keep us apart from us

I believe joy is analog not digital
It is all-natural not manufactured
And this is more of a feeling, not a fact,
but I kinda believe joy does not visit Florida much. . ..

I believe joy cannot be swallowed, injected, ingested,
snorted, nor mounted
Real joy believes everything,
is for your benefit,
...especially the pain

I believe joy is a horizon
One that will always seem beautiful,
and far in the distance when you look outside yourself for it
It will remain that way until the day
you look down and recognize
that you are a part of that distant sunset.
And someone else is looking at your accomplishments
in their horizon,
Both of you, a silhouette in your own pink, purple dusk,
looking at the other, saying to yourselves,
"I want what they have! There is my joy!"

[. . .]

I believe collectively, we have a Gotham complex
always secretly waiting for someone to save us,
but that is not the place where joy lives
Ask my 3yr old son,
I know Batman personally
And he told me as I am telling you,
Joy. . .is in the rescuing
Do not be ashamed of that

Receiving of the present is nice
but the giving of the gift. . .is joy
This is how we are built
Why we call children God's gifts.
The opportunity to serve, serves our spirits more than
    anything else

Let's be honest,
Children are the whiniest, clingiest,
most destructive things on this planet
And that's when they are still cute,
before puberty
But we love them anyway 'cause all we can do is give unto
    them,
pour into them
Ironically, by taking the focus away from us,
joy is placed within
I don't know how it works exactly
It may be magic
But I believe in magic

I believe in joy
I believe I wrote this poem
because I desperately needed to hear it
Because I keep looking for joy in places I know I will not find
    it. . .
            (Damn you Roscoe's Chicken and Waffles!)

I believe I was meant to stop here on the way to my sunset,
and that all of you, are part of my purpose

So here we are,
on this pink, purple horizon
Maybe for some of you,
it is bright yellowish blue
For others, your life is in the middle of its afternoon

And far in the distance,
are the people and the success that you covet
And in between that...
In between that...is the reason you were made
In between that, are the people we were meant to serve.
On the way to your horizon
Do not forget to look around you
In the dust
In the corners where the light can't quite reach
Believe it or not,
that is where your joy is
Right there, waiting to be served in your own communities
What a joy is it to know that real joy,
is closer than we could ever have imagined.

Skin Deep

There is a road we are all traveling
Partially paved
Mostly dangerous
The trees block out a lot of the sun,
but it still dares to break through from time to time
if you take a moment, to notice it
Yes. . .we are all headed in the same direction
The earth does not go in reverse
We might act like strangers
However, when we allow others to fall,
we all take two steps back
So this journey has taken us a while
Much too long if you ask me
And we are still not there yet
The strong repeatedly gets pushed down by the weak
And must quickly learn grace and survival
through extreme adversity

We are still breaking chains. . .
We know the constitution of a bully
Unloved and hurting. . .
With the ability to only see a person in 2D
Merely *skin deep*
Bullies are taught to reconcile the world by its differences
Not realizing that our fates are tied together by our souls. . .
And our bodies bounded together to this canvas called earth

This forever journey
This long walk to freedom
Tell me, whose map do we follow?
We were raised to believe in different doctrines, religions, topographies. . .
We can see the final destination in the distance
What I call a mountain, you call a hill, she calls a cliff. . .
Argue so much about the name, the darkness invades, and now it has become too late to reach it
Another day wasted,
another chalk outline created,
If this planet is a canvas,
This is not the type of art we wanted. . .

We are still breaking chains...
WE GET IT, you got an opinion
Get off the internet for a second...
You don't have to try to save America one post at a time
Just help me through this forest,
you get the food,
I'll collect the water,
we'll both enjoy the sunset,
watch the children dance and spin into their limitless
    possibilities
and we will all be just fine.

Quit trying to demand respect;
Instead, dedicate yourself to small acts of kindness
Micro progression...

Pouring out one cup of water a day on barren land,
means...Nothing
but have a city dedicated to doing it daily, we'd have a lake,
perhaps an ocean
And just like water,
bodies of kindness affects the climate
changes the conversation
So instead of digitally force-feeding people your perceived
    virtues
you are asking, "How can I make you feel valued?"

When you really think about it,
It is much too big.
This world and all of the pleasures inside of it are much too
    many
Quit trying to EVERYTHING, all the time baby
Quit tryin' to ALL THE TIME, all the time baby
Do not forsake the butterfly in your backyard
for want of the millions of stars in your sky
Sometimes stars are not to covet,
sometimes they are just to love from afar baby,
To say how wonderful is it that a God that took the time to
    make all them
was detailed enough to give me the mole I complain about

                                                          [...]

It's much too big baby
To hold them all in your precious arms
Some hugs, some hearts,
some personalities will just be too out of your reach
in the time you have to reach them baby
And that's ok.
Just know. . .
That's ok.

We are all chipped, flawed, broken, fractured,
fugazi, a bit phony, or are fucked up a tiny bit
and could *really* use some love right about now. . .
But first. . .be kind to yourself
Forgive the bruises
Kiss the cuts
Forgive the bruises
Kiss the cuts

A hip-hop philosopher mused,
"The deepest part of being black is being African,
the deepest part of being African is being human,
the deepest part of being human is being a part of God,
and the deepest part of being a part of God is being love. . .

When you view your fellow travelers on this road. . .
how deep is your vision?

There is a road we are all traveling
Partially paved, mostly dangerous
The trees block out a lot of the sun,
but it still dares to break through from time to time
If you take a moment, to notice it

Some folks on this journey are holding hands together,
others are lost and alone. . .

                                        . . .*Keep loving*

I can hear my own footsteps echo
and my heart awkwardly beating. . .

                                        . . .*Keep loving*

Sometimes I feel so alone amongst this pilgrimage of people

                                            ...Keep loving

But I know we are connected
and must meet on a level deeper than skin

                                            ...Keep loving

This path is hard on all of us
We cannot let the pain swallow us.

                                            ...Keep loving

Hold my hand, watch your step...
Keep *loving*...
Keep loving...
We are almost, there.

Acknowledgments

Some poems in this collection first appeared in the *San Diego Poetry Annual*.

Gratitude

I'd like to acknowledge Garden Oaks Press, Bill Harding in particular, who has been nothing but wonderful to work with and who believed in this project from the very beginning. Also, he was patient through the ice age it took to edit this work.

I'd also like to acknowledge Monkey C Media, and Jeniffer Thompson in particular. She and her team did an awesome job on the cover of this book.

I couldn't imagine a better team of collaborators all around.

Credits

Cover design: Jeniffer Thompson
monkeycmedia.com

About the Poet

GILL SOTU is a Navy veteran, poet, playwright, musician, DJ, and performing artist. He is a two time Grand Slam Poetry Champion, two time Raw Performing artist of the year, and a five time TEDx San Diego presenter. Currently, he is a teaching artist and a commissioned playwright with The Old Globe Theatre & The La Jolla Playhouse, a guest teaching artist with the SD School of Creative and Performing Arts and New Village Arts Theatre, and the official Poet in Residence for the San Diego Writer's Festival. 2 X Winner of Toastmaster's "Best Speaker Award" & "Inspirational Award" Gill has been featured multiple times on KPBS, The Union Tribune, The Voice Of San Diego, Fox 5 San Diego, The Coronado Times, and The VCReporter, as well as many other news outlets.

His screenplay *The History of Joy* in 2022 won two Gold Anthem Awards, was an Official Selection of the SoCal Film Awards and The San Diego Movie Awards, as well as the Silver Award for Best Drama at the Paris Film Awards; and was a Finalist at the Cannes World Film Festival. The poem he created and performed in for Project Clean Water won the Gold MarCom Award for advertising and has been shown at AMC & Regal Cinemas across San Diego County. As a DJ, Gill is a premiere DJ with MY DJs—one of the top wedding, private event and corporate DJ companies in SD, as well as one of the official DJ's for the SD Half Marathon. Gill is a former program director and teaching artist with Intrepid Theatre, creative director for TEDx San Diego, 2020 Artist-in-Residence for the Gainesville Creative Forces Art Summit, as well as the former Artist-in-Residence for The Jacobs Center for Neighborhood Innovation and Makers Church. He has been commissioned to produce original pieces for leading arts and community organizations such as: The San Diego Symphony, Classical Kids Live!, New Village Arts Theatre, The Unity Way, Feeding America, SD Fringe Fest, and the San Diego Opera, to name a few.

In 2023 Gill's newest play, *Saint George's Sword & Bow*, premiered internationally with the Toronto Symphony and nationally with the San Francisco Symphony, and is still touring with symphonies across North America.

www.ingramcontent.com/pod-product-compliance
Lightning Source LLC
Chambersburg PA
CBHW050914160426
43194CB00011B/2402